FROM EMPLOYEE TO FREELANCER

EXPERIENCES, HURDLES AND TIPS FOR SUCCESS

Ethan Clarke

TABLE OF CONTENTS

THE DECISION TO BECOME SELF-EMPLOYED

INITIAL CONSIDERATIONS

Deciding to become self-employed is a big step and requires careful consideration. This section discusses the initial thoughts and considerations that go into the decision to become self-employed.

THE MOTIVATION FOR SELF-EMPLOYMENT

Before you take the step into self-employment, it is important to be clear about your own motivations. Do you want more freedom and flexibility in your work arrangements? Do you have an innovative business idea that you want to realize? Or do you just want to be your own boss and take full responsibility for your professional life?

It is crucial to identify your goals and desires and to understand why you are interested in self-employment. This helps to make the right decisions and to make one's own path successful.

THE REALITY OF SELF-EMPLOYMENT

Before starting your own business, it is important to be aware of the reality of being self-employed. This includes acknowledging the challenges and risks that can come with being self-employed.

It is important to understand that self-employment is not always easy and that there can be ups and downs. It requires hard work, dedication, and a willingness to constantly evolve. It's also important to realize that if you're self-employed, you won't always have a stable income and that there may be times when you're financially insecure.

It is advisable to find out about the different aspects of self-employment and to exchange ideas with other self-employed people in order to get a realistic picture of self-employment.

DEVELOPING THE BUSINESS IDEA

A good business idea is the cornerstone of successful self-employment. This section is about how to get from an idea to implementation.

It's important to develop a business idea that fits your skills, interests, and goals. You should ask yourself what problems you can solve or what needs you can meet with your offer. Thorough market analysis and competitor analysis are also important to ensure that there is a market for what is on offer and that you can stand out from the competition.

It's also important to create a business plan that sets out the company's vision, goals, and strategy. The business plan serves as a guide for the implementation of the business idea and helps to plan the financial aspects.

THE LEGAL AND BUREAUCRATIC ASPECTS

Self-employment also brings with it legal and bureaucratic aspects that must be taken into account. This section discusses the first steps required to legally set up a business.

One of the most important steps is choosing the legal form of the company. There are various options such as sole proprietorship, limited liability company or UG, each of which has advantages and disadvantages. It is advisable to seek advice from a tax advisor or lawyer to find the best option for your business.

In addition, various registrations and registrations must be carried out, such as business registration, registration with the tax office and applying for a tax number. It is important to learn about the legal requirements and obligations to avoid possible problems and penalties.

The first considerations of self-employment are crucial for the success of the company. It is important to take time to understand your motivations, recognize the reality of being self-employed, develop a good business idea and pay attention to the legal aspects. With a solid foundation, you can successfully take the path to self-employment.

FROM IDEA TO IMPLEMENTATION

Deciding to start your own business is a big step and requires careful planning and preparation. In this section, we'll look at how to get from idea to implementation and what steps to follow.

FINDING THE IDEA

The first step on the way to self-employment is the development of a business idea. This idea should be based on your skills, interests, and experience. Think about what services or products you want to offer and how you can stand out from the competition. A great way to find ideas is to connect with other self-employed people, observe industry trends, and analyze potential customer needs.

MARKET ANALYSIS AND TARGET GROUP IDENTIFICATION

Once you have a business idea, it's important to analyze the market and determine your target audience. Research whether there are already similar offers and how much demand there is for your products or services. Identify your potential customers and analyze their needs to tailor your offer accordingly.

CREATE A BUSINESS PLAN

A business plan is an important tool for structuring your business idea and setting your goals. In your business plan, you should record your business strategy, your target audience, your marketing and sales strategy, and your financial projections. A well-thought-out business plan will not only help you define your own goals, but it can also be helpful when applying for funding or grants.

LEGAL FORM AND BUREAUCRATIC REQUIREMENTS

Before you can start your own business, you need to choose the appropriate legal form for your business and complete the necessary bureaucratic steps. Find out about the different legal forms such as sole proprietorship, limited liability company or UG and choose the one that best suits your needs. Apply for the necessary trade or commercial register entries and clarify tax issues with a tax advisor.

FINANCIAL PLANNING AND HEDGING

Financial planning is a crucial aspect of implementing your business idea. Create a realistic revenue and cost calculation and determine how you want to finance your business. You should also take into account any reserves for unforeseen expenses or a start-up period in which little or no income may be generated. Also think about your personal protection, such as health insurance or a retirement plan.

DEVELOP MARKETING AND SALES STRATEGY

To be successful as a freelancer, it's important to develop an effective marketing and sales strategy. Think about how you can attract potential customers and which channels you want to use to do so. Create a website or online shop, use social media platforms or rely on classic advertising measures such as flyers or advertisements. In addition, define your prices and conditions and think about how you can retain your customers in the long term.

IMPLEMENTATION AND LAUNCH OF YOUR OWN COMPANY

After you've made all the preparations, it's time to start your business and start implementing your business idea. Set up your workspace, create your stationery, and start acquiring customers. Be patient and give your business time to develop. Leverage your experience and learn from potential setbacks to continuously improve your business.

Implementing a business idea requires time, commitment and perseverance. Be prepared to take on challenges and react flexibly to change. However, with good planning and a clear vision, you can lay the foundation for successful self-employment.

BUREAUCRATIC BEGINNINGS

The path to self-employment begins with a multitude of bureaucratic tasks and formalities. This section covers the first steps necessary to start the process of starting your own business.

CHOICE OF LEGAL FORM

Before you become self-employed, you have to decide on a suitable legal form. There are various options such as sole proprietorship, GbR, GmbH or UG. Each legal form has its own advantages and disadvantages, which should be carefully considered. It is advisable to seek advice from a tax advisor or lawyer to make the best choice for your business.

BUSINESS REGISTRATION AND TAX NUMBER

Once a decision has been made on a legal form, it is necessary to register the business. This is usually done at the responsible trade office. It is necessary to provide information such as the name of the company, the areas of activity and the planned start date. After registering your business, you will receive a tax number, which is required for handling tax matters.

INSURANCE AND SOCIAL SECURITY CONTRIBUTIONS

As a self-employed person, you are responsible for your own social security. It is important to find out about the different types of insurance and choose the ones that suit your individual needs. These include, for example, health insurance, pension insurance and professional liability insurance. In addition, social security contributions such as health insurance and pension insurance must also be paid independently.

ACCOUNTING AND TAX RETURNS

As a self-employed person, you are obliged to keep proper accounting and to file tax returns regularly. It is advisable to familiarize yourself with the basics of accounting at an early stage or to hire a tax advisor to assist with the preparation of tax returns. In addition, all receipts and invoices should be carefully stored to ensure a smooth handling of tax matters.

INDUSTRIAL & LEGAL REGULATIONS

When it comes to self-employment, there are a large number of commercial and legal regulations that must be observed. These include, for example, data protection law, copyright law and competition law. It is important to learn about these regulations and ensure that your company meets all legal requirements.

FINANCING AND FUNDING OPPORTUNITIES

Starting your own business usually requires a certain amount of financial investment. It is important to realistically estimate the costs of setting up and running it and to plan for appropriate financing. Funding opportunities such as start-up grants or loans can also be taken advantage of. It is advisable to find out about the various funding programmes and, if necessary, to seek support in applying.

The bureaucratic beginnings of self-employment can seem overwhelming at first, but with the right preparation and support, these hurdles can be successfully overcome. It is important to deal with the legal and financial aspects at an early stage in order to lay a solid foundation for your own company. In the next sections, we'll cover other important topics that can make it easier to get started in the life of a freelancer and lead to success.

FINANCIAL ASPECTS

As a budding freelancer, it's important to consider the financial aspects of self-employment. In this section, we will look at the various financial considerations that go into deciding to become self-employed.

FINANCIAL PLANNING

Before you take the step into self-employment, it is advisable to carry out thorough financial planning. This includes analyzing your current financial situation as well as forecasting your future income and expenses as a freelancer. It's important to set realistic goals and allow for a financial buffer for unforeseen expenses.

PRICING

As a freelancer, you are responsible for setting your prices. It's important to know the value of your services and ask for reasonable prices. Consider your own costs, such as office rent, insurance, and taxes. A thorough market analysis can help you learn about the prices in your industry and set competitive prices.

TAXES AND INSURANCE

As a self-employed person, you will have to take care of your own taxes and insurance. Find out about the tax obligations and deadlines in your country and make sure you file all required tax returns on time. It may also be a good idea to sit down with a tax advisor to make sure you take advantage of all the tax benefits and don't make any mistakes.

In addition, you should find out about the different insurances that may be relevant for freelancers. These include, for example, professional liability insurance, health insurance and unemployment insurance. Each case is individual, so it is advisable to seek advice from an insurance advisor to find the right insurance solution for your needs.

ACCOUNTING

Proper bookkeeping is essential for freelancers. You should set up a system to track your income and expenses and keep all relevant receipts. Not only does this make it easier to file taxes, but it also gives you an overview of your financial situation and allows you to keep an eye on your business performance.

There are various accounting software and tools that can help you organize your finances. Find out about the different options and choose the system that best suits your needs.

FINANCIAL SECURITY

As a freelancer, you are responsible for your own income. It is important to build financial protection to bridge unforeseen financial bottlenecks. This can be achieved by creating an emergency fund or diversifying your sources of income. It is also advisable to build up reserves for long-term goals such as retirement planning.

WORKING WITH A FINANCIAL ADVISOR

If you feel insecure or need help with financial planning, you may want to consider working with a financial advisor. An expert can help you define your financial goals, develop a long-term financial strategy, and help you optimize your financial situation.

A financial advisor can also help you evaluate your investment options and help you plan for the future. It's important to find a trusted and knowledgeable financial advisor who understands your individual needs and goals.

RESULT

The financial aspects of self-employment are of great importance and should be carefully planned and considered. Thorough financial planning, setting reasonable prices, proper accounting, and financial security are critical to success as a freelancer. Don't hesitate to seek professional help to make sure you're on the right track and achieving your financial goals.

GETTING STARTED IN LIFE AS A FREELANCER

THE SEARCH FOR ORDERS

Finding jobs is one of the most important steps to getting started in the life of a freelancer. It is crucial to regularly find new projects to ensure a stable income and build your own client base. In this section, we will present various strategies and tips to successfully search for orders.

THE IMPORTANCE OF A PROFESSIONAL PORTFOLIO

A professional portfolio is an essential tool for any freelancer. It serves to give potential clients an overview of the work done and skills to date. A well-designed portfolio can make the difference between accepting an assignment or not. It is important to regularly update the portfolio and add new projects to demonstrate one's expertise.

USE ONLINE PLATFORMS AND JOB BOARDS

Online platforms and job boards offer a variety of ways to search for jobs. There are specialized platforms for different industries where freelancers can offer their services. It is advisable to register on several platforms and check for new projects regularly. It is important to pay attention to the reviews and references of other users in order to find reputable clients.

NETWORKING AND REFERRALS

A strong professional network can be a valuable source of new business. It's important to socialize and interact with other freelancers and potential clients. Networking events, industry meetings and conferences offer the opportunity to make new contacts and make yourself known. In addition, referrals from satisfied customers can be an effective way to generate new business.

PERSONAL INITIATIVE AND ACQUISITION

In addition to using online platforms and networking, it is also important to actively approach potential customers. Personal initiative and acquisition are decisive factors in winning new orders. This can be done, for example, by sending targeted inquiries or offering free initial consultations. It's important to learn about the potential customers and their needs in order to create tailored offers.

COOPERATIONS AND PARTNERSHIPS

Collaborations and partnerships with other freelancers or companies can be a great way to generate new business. By collaborating with other experts, larger projects can be realized that would not be feasible alone. It's important to connect with other freelancers and look for opportunities for collaborative projects.

THE IMPORTANCE OF TESTIMONIALS AND CUSTOMER REVIEWS

References and customer reviews play an important role in the search for new orders. Positive reviews and recommendations from satisfied customers can strengthen the trust of potential clients and increase the chances of new projects. It is advisable to ask customers for feedback and publish it on your own website or online platforms.

CONTINUOUS TRAINING AND SPECIALIZATION

In order to remain competitive and win new business, it is important to continuously educate yourself and specialize in certain areas of expertise. By acquiring new skills and knowledge, freelancers can expand their range of services and become more attractive to potential clients. It is advisable to regularly attend trainings, workshops or online courses to keep your finger on the pulse.

Finding jobs requires time, commitment, and a strategic approach. It is important to use different channels and actively seek new projects. With a professional portfolio, active acquisition, and a strong network, freelancers can successfully find new jobs and continue to grow their business.

BUILDING A NETWORK

A successful network is of great importance for freelancers. It not only allows access to new assignments, but also exchanges with like-minded people and the opportunity to learn from their experiences. This section covers various aspects of network building, from identifying potential contacts to maintaining and expanding the network.

IDENTIFICATION OF POTENTIAL CONTACTS

Before you can build a network, it's important to identify potential contacts. In doing so, you should look for possible contacts both in your own industry and in related areas. Here are some ways to find potential contacts:

Industry Events: Attend trade shows, conferences, and other events that take place in your industry. These offer an excellent opportunity to talk to other professionals and make contacts.

Online platforms: Use professional networks such as LinkedIn, Xing or freelancer platforms to find potential contacts. Browse the profiles of other freelancers or experts in your industry and get in touch.

Referrals: Ask your existing contacts if they can recommend someone to you. Often, your colleagues, friends, or family members know someone who works in your field or knows someone who can help you.

Social media: Use social media platforms such as Twitter, Facebook, or Instagram to connect with other professionals. Follow relevant people and companies, comment on their posts, and participate in discussions.

ESTABLISHING CONTACT AND BUILDING RELATIONSHIPS

After potential contacts have been identified, it is important to build a relationship with them. Here are some tips on how to successfully socialize:

Personalized messages: Make sure your outreach is personal and individualized. Avoid mass mailings or standard messages. Show interest in the person and their work and explain why you would like to get in touch with them.

Common Interests: Find common ground or common interests to talk about. This makes it easier to start the conversation and creates a connection between you and your potential contact.

Provide value: Think about how you can add value to your potential contact. This can be done, for example, by sharing relevant information, resources or experiences. By helping your contact, you build trust and strengthen the relationship.

Meetups and events: Try to arrange face-to-face meetings or virtual meetings to get to know your contacts better. This allows you to build a deeper relationship and discover potential synergies.

NETWORK MAINTENANCE AND EXPANSION

A network must be continuously maintained and expanded in order to be successful in the long term. Here are some tips on how to maintain and grow your network:

Regular exchange: Stay in regular contact with your contacts. Send them updates about your work, share relevant information, or congratulate them on successes. Show interest in their career and support them wherever possible.

Networking events: Continue to attend industry events to make new contacts and deepen existing relationships. Participate in discussions, give lectures, or offer yourself as a mentor. This shows your commitment and expertise.

Online interaction: Use social media platforms to stay connected with your contacts. Comment on their posts, share relevant content, and participate in discussions. This will help you stay visible and expand your network.

Referrals and collaborations: If you have worked successfully with a contact, do not hesitate to recommend them or suggest a collaboration. Not only does this strengthen the relationship, but it can also lead to new business opportunities.

Continuing education and events: Attend continuing education events or workshops to expand your knowledge and skills. Not only does this provide an opportunity to make new contacts, but it also strengthens your network as an expert in your field.

A well-built and maintained network can be invaluable for freelancers. It not only allows access to new assignments, but also exchanges with like-minded people and the opportunity to learn from their experiences. Invest time and energy in building and maintaining your network, and you'll feel the benefits in your professional development.

DEVELOPING A FREELANCER MINDSET

As a freelancer, it is crucial to develop a certain mindset in order to be successful in self-employment. A freelancer mindset is characterized by certain attitudes, mindsets, and behaviors that make it possible to overcome the challenges and opportunities of freelancing. In this section, we will look at how to develop such a mindset and give valuable tips on how to build a successful freelancer mindset.

THE IMPORTANCE OF SELF-CONFIDENCE AND SELF-MOTIVATION

Strong self-confidence is one of the most important prerequisites for success as a freelancer. As a self-employed person, you need to be able to believe in your own abilities and strengths and motivate yourself to keep going even in difficult times. Self-confidence can be strengthened by consciously acknowledging one's own successes and setting realistic goals. It's also important not to criticize yourself too much and learn from mistakes instead of being discouraged by them.

FLEXIBILITY AND ADAPTABILITY

As a freelancer, you are constantly confronted with change. Customer requirements may change, new technologies may emerge, and the market may evolve. Therefore, it is important to be flexible and adapt quickly to new situations. A freelancer mindset includes a willingness to learn new skills, evolve, and adapt to clients' needs. Flexibility allows a freelancer to react proactively to changes and take advantage of new opportunities.

SELF-ORGANIZATION AND TIME MANAGEMENT

As a freelancer, you are responsible for your own work organization. A successful freelancer mindset includes the ability to self-organize and manage time effectively. This includes setting clear goals, prioritizing tasks, and creating a structured work plan. It's important to keep yourself disciplined and minimize distractions to stay productive. Self-organization and time management are crucial to meeting deadlines and achieving a good work-life balance.

WILLINGNESS TO TAKE RISKS AND A SPIRIT OF INNOVATION

As a freelancer, it's important to take risks and be open to new ideas and innovations. A freelancer mindset includes the willingness to step out of the comfort zone and break new ground. This can mean opening up new markets, offering innovative solutions, or embracing new technologies. Risk-taking and innovative spirit allow a freelancer to stand out from the competition and discover new opportunities.

NETWORKING AND COLLABORATION

A successful freelancer mindset also includes the ability to build relationships and collaborate with others. Networking is an important part of freelancing life because it provides an opportunity to attract new clients, learn from others, and support each other. A freelancer should be open to collaborations, partnerships, and the exchange of knowledge and experience. Through networking and collaboration, a freelancer can expand their business and create new opportunities.

THE IMPORTANCE OF SELF-CARE AND BALANCE

As a freelancer, it's easy to get bogged down in your work and neglect your own health and personal well-being. However, a successful freelancer mindset includes the recognition that self-care and balance are of great importance. It is important to take regular breaks, take time for rest and relaxation, and take care of your own physical and mental health. Only if you are healthy and balanced yourself can you work successfully as a freelancer in the long term.

Developing a freelancer mindset takes time, practice, and a willingness to learn from mistakes. It is an ongoing process that allows a freelancer to continuously develop and succeed in self-employment. By working on your self-confidence, staying flexible, self-organizing, taking risks, building networks, and taking care of yourself, you can develop a strong freelancer mindset and achieve your goals as a freelancer.

THE BALANCE BETWEEN WORK AND LEISURE

As a freelancer, it's often a challenge to find the right balance between work and play. On the one hand, you want to be successful and advance your projects, but on the other hand, it is important to have enough time for relaxation and personal interests. In this section, we will look at different strategies and tips to achieve this balance.

THE IMPORTANCE OF WORK-LIFE BALANCE

Work-life balance is a concept that aims to create a balance between professional commitments and personal well-being. As a freelancer, it's especially important to find this balance, as you often work from home and the lines between work and play can become blurred.

A good work-life balance has many advantages. It helps reduce stress, increase productivity, and improve overall well-being. By allowing enough time for recreation and personal interests, you can maintain your energy and motivation and be successful in the long run.

TIME MANAGEMENT AND PRIORITIZATION

Effective time management is crucial to achieving the balance between work and play. It's important to set clear priorities and focus on the most important tasks. A great way to do this is to use to-do lists and blocks of time to structure the day.

It's also important to have realistic expectations and not want too much at once. Set clear goals and break down your work into smaller, doable tasks. Prioritize your tasks according to their urgency and importance, and if necessary, delegate tasks that don't necessarily need to be done by you.

THE IMPORTANCE OF BREAKS AND RECOVERY

Breaks and recovery are crucial to maintaining the balance between work and leisure. Take regular short breaks during your working hours to relax and recharge your batteries. Go for a walk, have a cup of tea, or just take a short break to refresh your mind.

In addition, it is important to regularly take longer breaks. Schedule regular days off or weekends where you can fully recover from work. Use this time to cultivate your hobbies, spend time with your loved ones, or just relax and unwind.

SET BOUNDARIES AND SWITCH OFF

As a freelancer, it's often difficult to leave work behind and switch off. There is always something to do and the temptation to work outside of regular working hours is great. However, it is important to set clear boundaries and consciously take time for yourself and your personal interests.

Try to set fixed hours and stick to them. After work, switch off your work equipment and devote yourself to your hobbies and interests. Create a separate workspace to physically separate work and leisure. By setting clear boundaries, you can effectively switch off and maintain the balance between work and play.

THE IMPORTANCE OF SELF-CARE

In addition to balancing work and play, it's also important to take care of yourself and take care of your physical and mental health. Make sure you get enough exercise, a healthy diet and enough sleep. Take time for relaxation techniques such as meditation or yoga to relieve stress and calm down.

Also, take care of your mental health. Take time for yourself regularly to reflect on your thoughts and feelings. Seek support from friends, family, or professional help if needed. By taking care of yourself and taking care of your health, you can be successful and happy as a freelancer in the long run.

FINDING THE BALANCE

Finding the balance between work and leisure is an individual challenge. Every freelancer has different needs and priorities. Experiment with different strategies and see what works best for you.

Remember that the balance between work and leisure is a continuous process. It requires regular reflection and adjustment to find and maintain the right balance. Be patient with yourself and give yourself permission to make mistakes and learn from them.

By maintaining the balance between work and play, you can not only be successful as a freelancer, but also live a full and happy life. Take the time to cultivate your personal interests and relationships and enjoy the freedom and flexibility that being a freelancer offers.

HURDLES ON THE ROAD TO SUCCESS

DEALING WITH UNCERTAINTY AND SELF-DOUBT

As a freelancer, it's normal to feel insecure and self-doubt. The step into self-employment is associated with many changes and challenges that can cause uncertainty. In this section, we'll look at how to deal with these feelings and how to overcome self-doubt to succeed as a freelancer.

THE IMPORTANCE OF SELF-CONFIDENCE

Self-confidence is an important factor in overcoming insecurity and self-doubt. It is important to believe in yourself and your abilities. Doubting yourself can have a negative impact on work and success. Therefore, it is important to strengthen one's self-confidence.

There are several ways to boost self-confidence. One way is to consciously remember past successes and remember that you have already successfully overcome many challenges. It can also be helpful to connect with other freelancers and learn from their experiences. You often find that others are also struggling with similar insecurities and self-doubt.

RECOGNIZING ONE'S OWN VALUE

A common reason for insecurity and self-doubt is feeling like you're not enough or don't have the value you demand as a freelancer. It's important to recognize your own value and realize that you have unique skills and experiences that are valuable to customers.

To recognize your own value, it can be helpful to make a list of your strengths and achievements. This list can serve as a reminder that you have valuable skills and have already achieved success. It can also be helpful to get feedback from clients or other freelancers to learn how they perceive your work.

DEALING WITH UNCERTAINTY

Uncertainty is a natural part of being a freelancer. It's important to accept that there will always be uncertainties and that you can't control everything. Instead of being paralyzed by uncertainty, you can learn to deal with it and use it as an opportunity for personal and professional growth.

One way to deal with uncertainty is to be aware that mistakes and setbacks are part of the learning process. Every freelancer makes mistakes and has setbacks, but it's important to learn from them and grow. It can also be helpful to focus on your own strengths and successes to boost confidence and reduce uncertainty.

SEEK SUPPORT

It is important to recognize that you are not alone and that there is support. It can be helpful to exchange ideas with other freelancers and learn from their experiences. There are also various networks and organizations that offer support for freelancers, such as mentoring programs or workshops.

It can also be helpful to see a coach or therapist to help you deal with uncertainty and self-doubt. A coach can help to identify one's own strengths and abilities and to strengthen self-confidence. A therapist can help identify and change negative thought patterns.

MOTIVATE YOURSELF

As a freelancer, you are your own boss and you have to motivate yourself. It's important to set clear goals and regularly remind yourself why you decided to become self-employed. It can also be helpful to treat yourself to small rewards on a regular basis to keep you motivated.

It's also important not to criticize yourself too harshly and to allow yourself to make mistakes. Everyone has a bad day or makes mistakes, but that doesn't mean you're a bad freelancer. It is important to accept yourself and allow yourself to be human.

Overall, it's normal to feel insecurity and self-doubt as a freelancer. It's important to acknowledge and accept these feelings, but at the same time work on building confidence and dealing with uncertainty. With the right attitude and support, you can overcome these hurdles and be successful as a freelancer.

CUSTOMER ACQUISITION AND CONTRACT NEGOTIATIONS

Client acquisition and contract negotiations are crucial steps on the way to success as a freelancer. In this section, we'll look at how to find potential clients, how to convince them, and how to conduct successful contract negotiations.

THE SEARCH FOR POTENTIAL CUSTOMERS

Finding potential clients can be challenging, especially if you're just starting out as a freelancer. However, there are several ways to find potential customers and get them to know you.

One way is to use your network. Talk to friends, family, and former colleagues about being self-employed and ask them if they know anyone who needs your services. Often, personal recommendations can make it easier to get started.

Another option is to have an online presence. Create a professional website where you showcase your services and references. Also use social media platforms such as LinkedIn, Xing or Instagram to present yourself and your work. Publish regular posts that showcase your expertise and appeal to potential customers.

In addition, you can also search for jobs on job portals and freelancer platforms. Here you can apply for projects or present your profile to be found by potential clients. However, make sure that you stand out from the crowd and make your unique selling points clear.

CONVINCING PRESENTATION OF YOUR SERVICES

Once you've found potential clients, it's important to convince them of your services. A compelling presentation can make all the difference and secure your job.

Start by describing your services in a clear and understandable way. Highlight what added value you can offer the customer and why you are the right choice. Show references and experience to underline your competence.

In addition, it is important to respond to the customer's needs. Listen carefully and ask specific questions to find out exactly what the customer is looking for. Customize your presentation accordingly and show how you can meet their needs.

Another important aspect is to build trust. Clients want to make sure that they are working with a reliable and professional freelancer. Therefore, show your reliability by meeting deadlines, maintaining clear communication, and delivering your work to a high standard.

SUCCESSFUL CONTRACT NEGOTIATIONS

Once you've convinced the client of your services, it's a matter of signing a contract. Contract negotiations can sometimes be challenging, but with the right preparation and strategy, you can be successful.

First of all, it is important to clearly define the scope of the work and the conditions. Clarify all the important details such as the time frame, payment, any additional benefits, and the rights to your work. Make sure both sides have a clear understanding of what is expected.

It is also advisable to draw up a written contract. This should include all agreements and terms to avoid misunderstandings. If you're unsure, you can consult a lawyer to review the contract and make sure it's legally binding.

During negotiations, it's important to be confident and represent your prices and conditions. However, be willing to compromise and be flexible to create a win-win situation for both parties.

Finally, it is important to build a good relationship with the customer. Maintain open and transparent communication throughout the project and make sure the client is happy with your work. Positive cooperation can lead to further orders and recommendations.

RESULT

Client acquisition and contract negotiations are crucial steps on the way to success as a freelancer. By convincing potential customers and conducting successful contract negotiations, you lay the foundation for successful self-employment. Use your network, present yourself online and be persuasive in your presentation. Prepare well for contract negotiations and build a good relationship with the customer. With these strategies, you can significantly increase your chances of success as a freelancer.

TIME MANAGEMENT AND ORGANIZATION

As a freelancer, it's crucial to have effective time management and good organization. Without these skills, it can be difficult to keep track of projects and tasks and get the job done efficiently. In this section, we will look at different strategies and techniques that can help you use your time effectively and organize your work in the best possible way.

SETTING PRIORITIES

One of the most important time management skills is the ability to prioritize. As a freelancer, you often have multiple projects and tasks at the same time, and it's important to know which of them are the highest priority. One way to prioritize is to use a priority list. This list contains all your tasks and projects and assigns them a priority level. This way, you'll always know which tasks need to be done first and which can be done later.

CREATING TIME BLOCKS

Another effective method of time management is to create blocks of time. Certain periods of time are reserved for specific tasks or projects. By dividing your time into blocks, you can ensure that you have enough time for each task and don't get distracted by other tasks. For example, you could set aside two hours each morning to work on emails and three hours in the afternoon to work on a particular project. By dividing your time into blocks, you can better structure your work and be more productive.

USE TO-DO LISTS

To-do lists are a simple yet effective tool to organize your tasks. You can either keep a physical paper list or use a digital to-do list on your computer or smartphone. Write down all your tasks and mark them when they're done. To-do lists help you keep track of your tasks and make sure nothing gets forgotten. You can also prioritize by organizing your tasks by urgency.

DELEGATING AND OUTSOURCING

As a freelancer, you may not always have enough time to complete all the tasks yourself. In such cases, it is important to learn to delegate or outsource tasks. Identify tasks that can be done by others and consider whether it makes sense to pass them on to other people or companies. This can help you make better use of your time and focus on the tasks that only you can do.

CREATING AN EFFECTIVE WORK ENVIRONMENT

A well-organized and tidy work environment can have a positive effect on your productivity and concentration. Take the time to organize your workspace and make sure you have everything you need to do your job. Remove distractions such as messy desks or loud noises and create a quiet and pleasant work environment. This can help you focus better and do your job more efficiently.

SCHEDULE TIME FOR BREAKS

It's important to incorporate regular breaks into your workday. Breaks help you recover, recharge your energy, and maintain your concentration. Schedule short breaks between tasks and make time for longer breaks to relax and recharge. Use these breaks to get some exercise, get some fresh air, or just relax. By scheduling breaks into your workday, you can increase your productivity and achieve a better work-life balance.

LEVERAGING TECHNOLOGY

Proper use of technology can help you use your time effectively and better organize your work. There are many tools and apps that can help you manage your tasks, plan your time, and organize your work. Find out which tools suit you best and use them to get your work done more efficiently. For example, you can use project management software to manage your projects or a time tracking app to track your working hours.

MAINTAIN FLEXIBILITY

While good organization and effective time management are important, it's also important to stay flexible. As a freelancer, priorities and tasks can change quickly, and it's important to adapt to new situations. Be prepared to adjust your plans and reorganize your time as new tasks or projects arise. Flexibility is an important quality to be successful as a freelancer.

RESULT

Effective time management and good organization are crucial for success as a freelancer. By prioritizing, creating blocks of time, using to-do lists, delegating tasks, creating an effective work environment, scheduling regular breaks, leveraging technology, and staying flexible, you can use your time efficiently and organize your work in the best possible way. Take the time to improve your time management skills and find out which strategies and techniques suit you best. With a good organization, you can increase your productivity, reduce stress, and live a successful freelance life.

MISTAKES AND SETBACKS AS AN OPPORTUNITY

As a freelancer, it's inevitable that you'll also face mistakes and setbacks on the road to success. But instead of seeing them as obstacles, they should be seen as opportunities to grow and develop. In this section, we'll look at the importance of mistakes and setbacks and how to use them as valuable lessons.

THE POSITIVE ATTITUDE TOWARDS MISTAKES

Mistakes are part of life as a freelancer and should not be seen as failures. Rather, they are a natural part of the learning process and provide an opportunity to learn from them and improve. It's important to develop a positive attitude towards mistakes and see them as valuable experiences. By reflecting and analyzing your mistakes, you can figure out what went wrong and how you can do better in the future.

THE ART OF DEALING WITH SETBACKS

Setbacks are also part of life as a freelancer. It can happen that you don't get a job, a project fails, or you are faced with financial difficulties.

In such moments, it is important not to lose heart and not to be discouraged. Instead, you should use setbacks as an opportunity to rethink and improve your skills and strategies. You can ask yourself what went wrong and how to do it differently in the future. Setbacks can also serve to discover new paths and develop further.

DRAWING LESSONS FROM MISTAKES AND SETBACKS

In order to learn from mistakes and setbacks, it is important to reflect and analyze them. One should take the time to understand what went wrong and what factors contributed to it. It can be helpful to ask yourself critical questions and to be honest with yourself. What could have been done differently? What skills or knowledge are you missing? What strategies didn't work? By answering these questions, you can learn valuable lessons for the future and improve the way you work.

THE IMPORTANCE OF GROWTH

Mistakes and setbacks are not only opportunities to learn from them, but also to grow personally. By facing the challenges and learning from your mistakes, you can expand your skills and knowledge. You learn to be more flexible and adaptable and develop a positive attitude towards change. The growth you experience through mistakes and setbacks can make you a better freelancer and pave the way to success.

THE SUPPORT OF MENTORS AND NETWORKS

When dealing with mistakes and setbacks, it can be helpful to seek support from mentors and other freelancers. Mentors can share valuable advice and experience and help you learn from your mistakes. Networks offer the opportunity to exchange ideas with like-minded people and benefit from their experiences. By exchanging ideas with others, you can gain new perspectives and discover new solutions.

THE IMPORTANCE OF RESILIENCE

Resilience, or the ability to deal with and recover from setbacks, is an important trait for freelancers. It is important not to be discouraged by mistakes and setbacks, but to get back up and move on. Resilience can be developed through various strategies and techniques, such as maintaining a positive attitude, setting realistic goals, and maintaining a healthy lifestyle.

THE OPPORTUNITY FOR REALIGNMENT

Mistakes and setbacks can also provide an opportunity for realignment. If a particular approach didn't work, you can explore new ways and find alternative solutions. You can rethink your goals and strategies and realign yourself if necessary. Mistakes and setbacks can help you discover new opportunities and redefine your path as a freelancer.

THE IMPORTANCE OF PERSEVERANCE

Dealing with mistakes and setbacks requires perseverance. It is important not to give up and to continue to stick to your goals. Even though it can be difficult, don't get discouraged and believe in yourself. Perseverance is an important trait to overcome the challenges of being a freelancer and ultimately succeed.

Mistakes and setbacks are part of life as a freelancer. By developing a positive attitude towards them, learning from them, and seeing them as opportunities for personal and professional growth, you can pave your way to success. It is important not to be discouraged by mistakes and setbacks, but to accept them as part of the learning process and move on. With perseverance, resilience, and the support of mentors and networks, you can overcome the hurdles on the road to success and grow and thrive as a freelancer.

FINANCIAL CHALLENGES

As a freelancer, you face various financial challenges that need to be overcome. Unlike an employee, as a self-employed person, you do not have a regular salary receipt and have to take care of your finances yourself. In this section, we'll look at the financial aspects of self-employment and give you some tips on how to successfully overcome these challenges.

BUDGET PLANNING AND INCOME SECURITY

As a freelancer, it's important to create a realistic budget and plan your income and expenses carefully. Since your income may not be constant, you should build up reserves for more financially difficult times. It is advisable to have at least three to six months of expenses available as an emergency fund.

To increase your income security, you should consider different sources of income. For example, depending on your industry, you can take on different assignments, get involved in long-term projects, or take advantage of passive income streams such as selling digital products or participating in affiliate marketing programs.

TAXES AND ACCOUNTING

As a self-employed person, you are responsible for your own accounting and tax returns. It is important to familiarize yourself with the tax requirements at an early stage and, if necessary, to seek professional support from a tax advisor. Be sure to properly document all your income and expenses and make your tax payments on time to avoid potential penalties.

In addition, you should find out about possible tax benefits and deductions that are available to you as a self-employed person. This can help you minimize your tax burden and keep more money in your pocket.

PRICING AND NEGOTIATION

Setting your prices as a freelancer can be challenging. You want to be competitive while making a reasonable profit. It's important to consider your cost, time, and the value of your services or products. Research the market and compare the prices of similar services or products to get realistic pricing.

When negotiating with clients, it's important to be confident and communicate the value of your work. Be prepared to negotiate prices and terms, but keep your financial goals in mind. It's better to turn down an order that doesn't meet your financial expectations than to offer your services at low prices and jeopardize your profitability.

INSURANCE AND RETIREMENT PROVISION

As a self-employed person, you have to take care of your own insurance and retirement provision. Check your existing insurance policies and make sure you are adequately covered. This includes health insurance, professional indemnity insurance and, if applicable, public liability insurance.

In addition, you should think about your retirement provision at an early stage. As a self-employed person, you do not have an employer's contribution to the pension insurance and therefore have to provide for your own financial security in old age. Find out about various options for retirement provision, such as private pension insurance or setting up your own company pension scheme.

FINANCIAL EDUCATION AND DEVELOPMENT

In order to successfully overcome the financial challenges of self-employment, it is important to continuously educate yourself and improve your financial literacy. Learn about topics such as accounting, taxes, investments, and financial planning. Read books, attend training sessions or webinars, and seek the advice of experts.

By improving your financial literacy, you can make informed decisions and improve your financial situation in the long run. Take regular time to review your finances, adjust your goals, and adjust your strategies accordingly.

SUMMARY

Self-employment comes with financial challenges that need to be overcome. Through careful budget planning, attention to tax requirements, appropriate pricing, insurance and continuous training, you can successfully overcome these challenges. Be proactive and take charge of your financial situation to succeed as a freelancer.

DEALING WITH STRESS AND PRESSURE

As a freelancer, it's inevitable that you'll face stress and pressure every now and then. The responsibility for one's own success and the constant search for new orders can become a burden. In this section, we will look at how best to deal with stress and pressure in order to stay successful and healthy in the long term.

RECOGNISING AND UNDERSTANDING STRESS

Stress is a natural reaction of the body to challenging situations. It is important to recognize and understand stress early on in order to be able to respond appropriately. Everyone reacts differently to stress, so it's important to identify your own stress triggers. These can be, for example, tight deadlines, difficult customers or financial uncertainty. By being aware of which situations trigger stress, you can be better prepared for them and develop strategies to deal with them.

STRESS MANAGEMENT TECHNIQUES

There are several techniques to deal with and manage stress. Everyone has their own preferences, so it's important to find the techniques that suit you best. Here are some best practices for managing stress:

Relaxation techniques: Relaxation techniques such as meditation, yoga, or breathing exercises can help reduce stress and calm the mind. Taking regular breaks and consciously taking time to relax is important to lower stress levels.

Sports and physical activity: Physical activity is an effective way to reduce stress. Exercise releases endorphins, which can increase well-being and reduce stress. It is important to exercise regularly and get enough exercise to keep the body and mind healthy.

Time management: Good organization and effective time management can help reduce stress. By setting priorities, structuring tasks, and setting realistic goals, you can better manage your day-to-day work and avoid stress.

Seeking support: It's important not to be afraid to ask for help and to seek support when stress gets too high. This can be, for example, exchanging ideas with other freelancers who have had similar experiences, or bringing in a coach or therapist to help them cope with stress.

SELF-CARE AND BALANCE

In order to remain successful and healthy in the long term, it is important to take care of yourself and provide a balance. Here are some self-care tips:

Take breaks: Taking regular breaks and taking time for rest and relaxation is essential to prevent stress. Short breaks should also be planned during work to relieve the mind and recharge your batteries.

Set boundaries: It's important to set clear boundaries and not overwhelm yourself. By setting realistic working hours and not taking on too many tasks at once, you can avoid stress and maintain a healthy work-life balance.

Cultivate hobbies and interests: Taking time for hobbies and interests is a great way to clear your head and provide a balance. Whether it's reading a book, playing a sport, or catching up with friends, it's important to make time for your interests and not just focus on work.

Healthy lifestyle: A healthy diet, adequate sleep and regular exercise are important factors in preventing stress and maintaining physical and mental health. It is important to take care of yourself and consciously make time for healthy habits.

MANAGING THE PRESSURE

In addition to stress, the pressure that comes with being self-employed can also be stressful. Here are some tips to cope with the pressure:

Realistic expectations: It's important to have realistic expectations of yourself and your goals. Things aren't always going to go perfectly right away, and that's okay. By setting realistic goals and not putting too much pressure on yourself, you can reduce the pressure and focus on the path to success.

Positive attitude: A positive attitude can help manage pressure and deal with setbacks. By focusing on your own strengths and successes and not getting too discouraged by failures, you can reduce the pressure and stay motivated.

Network and support: A strong network of like-minded people and supporters can help manage the pressure. Sharing with other freelancers, sharing experiences, and supporting each other can be a great help in reducing pressure and gaining new perspectives.

Change of perspective: Sometimes it can be helpful to change your perspective and look at things from a different perspective. By being aware that not everything has to be perfect and that setbacks also offer opportunities, you can reduce the pressure and find new solutions.

Dealing with stress and pressure is an individual challenge that each freelancer has to overcome in their own way. By becoming aware of which techniques and strategies suit you best, you can stay successful and healthy in the long term. It's important to take care of yourself, seek support, and don't put too much pressure on yourself.

MOMENTS OF HAPPINESS AND DOWNSIDES

ACHIEVEMENTS AND MILESTONES

As a freelancer, there are many successes and milestones that you can achieve on your way to self-employment. These successes are not only important for one's own self-confidence, but also for the further development of one's own business. In this section, we'll highlight some of the key achievements and milestones freelancers can achieve on their path to success.

THE FIRST ORDER

The first assignment as a freelancer is a big milestone and an important success. It's the moment when you prove that you can be successful as a self-employed person. However, the first assignment can also be associated with uncertainty and nervousness. It is important to rely on your abilities and appear confident. As soon as the first order is successfully completed, you can be proud of yourself and look forward to further orders.

THE FIRST POSITIVE CUSTOMER REVIEW

A positive customer review is a great achievement for any freelancer. It shows that you've done a good job and that the client is happy with the results. Positive customer reviews are not only a sign of the quality of one's work, but also a valuable reference for future customers. They can help gain the trust of potential customers and further grow one's business.

THE FIRST MAJOR CONTRACT AWARD

When you get a bigger job as a freelancer, it's a great achievement and an important milestone. Larger jobs often mean more work and responsibility, but they also offer the opportunity to grow and learn new skills. The successful completion of a larger order can boost one's self-confidence and further strengthen the trust of customers in one's own work.

THE FIRST LONG-TERM CUSTOMER RELATIONSHIP

A long-term client relationship is a great success for any freelancer. It shows that you are not only doing a good job, but that you have also gained the trust of the customer. Long-term customer relationships offer not only financial security, but also the opportunity to develop and grow together with the customer. They are a sign of the quality of one's own work and a valuable reference for future customers.

THE FIRST POSITIVE PRESS OR AWARD

When you receive positive press or an award as a freelancer, it's a great achievement and an important milestone. Positive press or awards can make your business better known and increase the trust of potential customers. They are also an acknowledgement of the quality of one's work and a reward for the hard work and dedication one has invested in one's business.

THE FIRST EMPLOYEE

If you are so successful as a freelancer that you decide to hire an employee, that is a great achievement and an important milestone. Hiring employees allows you to continue to grow your business and take on more business. It's also a sign that you're successful as a freelancer and that your business is growing.

THE FIRST MAJOR INVESTMENT

If you've made enough money as a freelancer to make a larger investment, that's a huge achievement and an important milestone. Larger investments can help to further grow one's business and create new opportunities. They are also a sign that you are successful as a freelancer and that your business is growing.

THE FIRST POSITIVE FEEDBACK FROM CUSTOMERS

Positive feedback from clients is a great success for any freelancer. They show that you have done a good job and that customers are satisfied with the results. Positive feedback is not only a sign of the quality of one's own work, but also a valuable reference for future customers. They can help to gain the trust of potential customers and further expand your own business.

YOUR FIRST OWN EVENT OR CONFERENCE

Once you have gained enough experience and knowledge as a freelancer, you can decide to organize your own event or conference. This is a huge achievement and an important milestone as it shows that as a freelancer you are recognized as an expert and that you are able to inspire and motivate other people. Hosting your own event or conference can also help expand your network and create new business opportunities.

THE ACHIEVEMENT OF PERSONAL GOALS

As a freelancer, it's important to set personal goals and achieve them. Achieving personal goals is a great achievement and an important milestone as it shows that as a freelancer you are capable of achieving your dreams and goals. Personal goals can be, for example, starting your own business, opening your own office or participating in an international conference. Achieving personal goals can boost one's self-confidence and increase one's sense of achievement and satisfaction.

These successes and milestones are just a few examples of the many opportunities freelancers can achieve on their path to success. Every freelancer has their own goals and dreams, and it's important to be aware of them and work towards them. With hard work, dedication, and the right attitude, freelancers can achieve their goals and succeed.

THE FREEDOM OF BEING A FREELANCER

Working as a freelancer means having the freedom to be your own boss and to determine your own working hours and locations. This freedom is one of the main reasons why many people choose to be self-employed. In this section, we'll take a closer look at the freedom of freelancing and the pros and cons of this way of working.

THE BENEFITS OF FREEDOM

The freedom to work as a freelancer offers numerous advantages. One of the most obvious advantages is the flexibility in working hours. As a freelancer, you can decide for yourself when you work and when you take time off. You are not bound to fixed working hours and can adapt your work to your personal needs and preferences. This flexibility allows you to find a balance between work and leisure time and use your working time effectively.

Another benefit of the freedom of being a freelancer is the ability to work from anywhere. You are not tied to a specific place of work and can choose your workplace according to your needs and preferences. Whether you prefer to work from home, in a café or in a coworking space – as a freelancer you have the freedom to choose where you work. This flexibility allows you to design your work environment so that you can work productively and creatively.

In addition, the freedom of being a freelancer offers the opportunity to decide for yourself the type of work you take on. You can choose projects that interest you and match your skills. As a freelancer, you have the freedom to specialize in specific industries or areas of responsibility and to develop yourself. This freedom allows you to pursue your professional goals and steer your career in the direction you want.

THE CHALLENGES OF FREEDOM

While there are many benefits to the freedom of freelancing, there are also challenges that come with it. One of the biggest challenges is self-organization. As a freelancer, you are responsible for your own work scheduling and must ensure that you complete your tasks on time. This personal responsibility requires discipline and good time management skills. It can sometimes be difficult to find the balance between work and leisure and to motivate yourself, especially if there are no fixed working hours.

Another challenge of freedom as a freelancer is loneliness and isolation. Since you often work alone, you miss the social contact and exchange with colleagues. It can be difficult to motivate yourself and stay productive when there's no one around to support you or give you feedback. It's important to develop strategies to deal with this loneliness, such as meeting with other freelancers on a regular basis or attending networking events.

In addition, the freedom of being a freelancer can also bring financial insecurity. As a freelancer, you're responsible for your own job acquisition and need to make sure you have enough projects to make a living. It can be difficult to build a stable customer base and receive orders on a regular basis. It requires good self-marketing and the ability to build and maintain customer relationships.

FINDING THE BALANCE

To take full advantage of the freedom of freelancing, it's important to find the right balance. It's about reaping the benefits of freedom while overcoming the challenges. Good self-organization and time management skills are crucial to work productively and effectively. It can be helpful to set fixed hours and create a structured work schedule.

In addition, it is important to develop strategies to deal with loneliness and isolation. This can mean regularly exchanging ideas with other freelancers, joining a coworking space or participating in networking events. Connecting with like-minded people can not only alleviate loneliness, but also open up new professional opportunities.

Finally, it's important to ensure financial security as a freelancer. This means building up a stable customer base and acquiring new orders on a regular basis. Effective self-marketing and the ability to build and maintain customer relationships are crucial. It can also be helpful to build up financial reserves to bridge financial bottlenecks.

Overall, the freedom of freelancing offers many opportunities, but also challenges. By taking advantage of the benefits, overcoming the challenges, and finding the right balance, you can work successfully and fulfilledly as a freelancer.

LONELINESS AND ISOLATION

As a freelancer, it can happen that you feel lonely and isolated. Unlike a white-collar job, where you work with colleagues on a daily basis, as a freelancer you often work alone. This loneliness can be both physical and emotional and can have various effects.

PHYSICAL LONELINESS

Physical loneliness occurs when you work alone in your home office all day, without the opportunity to interact with other people. It can feel like a kind of prison where you sit alone in front of the computer all day. The lack of social interactions can lead to feelings of isolation and affect motivation and productivity.

There are several ways to overcome physical loneliness. One option is to use coworking spaces where freelancers can collaborate and exchange ideas. These places of work offer the opportunity to connect with other people and build a network. Regular visits to coworking spaces can help reduce loneliness and strengthen a sense of belonging.

Another way to combat physical loneliness is to participate in networking events or meetups. These events offer the opportunity to meet and exchange ideas with other freelancers and potential clients. By building a network, you can not only generate new orders, but also reduce the feeling of loneliness.

EMOTIONAL LONELINESS

In addition to physical loneliness, emotional loneliness can also occur. As a freelancer, you often don't have anyone with whom you can discuss professional challenges or successes. There is a lack of direct contact with colleagues that is present in an employment relationship. This can lead to a feeling of isolation and abandonment.

To deal with emotional loneliness, it's important to build a support network. This network can consist of other freelancers, mentors, or friends who can help you with professional questions or problems. Sharing with like-minded people can help reduce feelings of loneliness and gain new perspectives.

In addition, it is important to reflect on yourself and realize that loneliness and isolation can be part of being a freelancer. By being aware of this fact, you can develop strategies to deal with it. This may include, for example, regular breaks and social activities to maintain contact with other people.

THE IMPORTANCE OF FEEDBACK AND RECOGNITION

Loneliness and isolation can also make you feel insecure and doubt yourself. Without regular feedback from colleagues or superiors, it can be difficult to gauge one's progress and performance. The lack of recognition can affect motivation and lead to self-doubt.

To counteract this problem, it is important to give yourself feedback and reflect on yourself regularly. You can set goals and review them regularly to measure your progress. In addition, it can be helpful to build a support network that gives you feedback and recognition. This network can consist of colleagues, mentors, or friends who help you assess your performance.

It's also important to give yourself credit and realize that as a freelancer you overcome many challenges and achieve success. By focusing on your strengths and achievements, you can reduce feelings of loneliness and isolation and boost self-confidence.

Overall, it's important to be aware of loneliness and isolation as a freelancer and develop strategies to deal with it. By building a support network, regularly exchanging ideas with other freelancers and consciously reflecting on yourself, you can reduce the feeling of loneliness and lead a successful freelance life.

THE IMPORTANCE OF FEEDBACK AND RECOGNITION

Feedback and recognition play a crucial role in a freelancer's success and well-being. In this section, we'll take a closer look at the importance of feedback and recognition and how they affect different aspects of being a freelancer.

FEEDBACK AS A DEVELOPMENT OPPORTUNITY

Feedback is a valuable tool for growing as a freelancer. It allows us to identify our strengths and weaknesses and improve our skills. By getting constructive feedback from clients, colleagues, or mentors, we can optimize the way we work and become more professional.

It's important to see feedback not as criticism or attack, but as an opportunity for improvement. By being open to feedback and seeing it as a learning opportunity, we can expand our skills and knowledge. Others' feedback can open up new perspectives and help us take our work to a higher level.

THE IMPORTANCE OF RECOGNITION

Recognition is another important aspect for freelancers. It makes us feel valued and respected. When our work is recognized, it not only boosts our confidence, but also motivates us to continue to do our best.

Recognition can be done in a number of ways. On the one hand, we can receive recognition from our customers if they are satisfied with our work and recommend us to others. On the other hand, we can also receive recognition from our colleagues and the freelancer community if we actively participate and share our knowledge.

It is important that we also give ourselves recognition. By celebrating our successes and praising ourselves for our accomplishments, we boost our confidence and motivation. Self-recognition is an important part of the self-reliance process and helps us to motivate ourselves and continue to work hard.

FEEDBACK AND RECOGNITION AS THE BASIS FOR CUSTOMER LOYALTY

Feedback and recognition also play a crucial role in customer retention. When we listen to our customers and listen to their feedback, we show them that we take their needs seriously and are willing to adapt. This strengthens trust and relationship with our customers and can lead to long-term business relationships.

Recognition is also an important factor in customer loyalty. By showing our clients that we value their work and thanking them for working with them, they feel valued and will be more willing to recommend us to others or use our services again.

THE ROLE OF FEEDBACK AND RECOGNITION IN WELL-BEING

Feedback and recognition also have a direct impact on our personal well-being as freelancers. When we regularly receive positive feedback and recognition for our work, it boosts our self-esteem and overall well-being.

On the other hand, a lack of feedback or negative feedback can lead to insecurity and self-doubt. It's important that we don't get too discouraged by negative feedback, but see it as an opportunity to improve. By focusing on our strengths and using constructive feedback, we can overcome our self-doubt and boost our self-confidence.

THE SEARCH FOR FEEDBACK AND RECOGNITION

To get feedback and recognition, it's important to actively seek it. We may ask our clients for feedback by asking them about their satisfaction with our work or by asking them for constructive criticism. We can also build a network of colleagues and mentors who can give us feedback on a regular basis.

We can earn recognition by attending industry events, sharing our knowledge in the freelancer community, or collaborating with other freelancers. By actively participating in the community and sharing our knowledge, we can position ourselves as an expert and receive recognition from other freelancers.

It's important that we don't just rely on external sources of feedback and recognition, but also acknowledge our own successes and progress. By regularly taking time to reflect on our successes and praise ourselves, we can boost our confidence and increase our well-being.

Feedback and recognition are crucial factors in a freelancer's success and well-being. By being open to feedback, actively seeking recognition, and giving ourselves recognition, we can improve our skills, retain customers, and increase our personal well-being.

HEALTHY SELF-RELIANCE

PHYSICAL AND MENTAL HEALTH

As a freelancer, it is of great importance to take care of your physical and mental health. Self-employment brings with it a lot of freedom, but also a high level of responsibility and burden. In this section, we'll cover important aspects that will help you work healthily and successfully as a freelancer.

THE IMPORTANCE OF PHYSICAL HEALTH

Physical health is the basis for a successful working life. As a freelancer, you are your own boss and are responsible for your company. In order to be able to take on this responsibility, it is important to pay attention to your physical condition. Here are some tips that can help you:

Regular exercise: As a freelancer, you often spend a lot of time at your desk. It's important to incorporate regular exercise into your daily routine. Take breaks, go for a walk, or exercise to keep your body fit.

Ergonomic workstation: Make sure that your workplace is ergonomically designed. A good sitting posture and the correct positioning of the screen, keyboard and mouse can prevent back and neck problems.

Healthy eating: A balanced diet is essential for your physical health. Make sure that you eat a balanced and varied diet and drink enough fluids.

Get enough sleep: Sleep is important to regenerate your body and recharge your batteries for the next day at work. Make sure you get enough sleep and get enough time to recover.

THE IMPORTANCE OF MENTAL HEALTH

In addition to physical health, mental health is also of great importance. As a freelancer, you are often alone and have to make a lot of decisions. Here are some tips that can help you boost your mental health:

Stress management: Stress is a natural companion of being a freelancer. It's important to develop effective strategies to deal with stress. Find out which methods help you reduce stress, such as meditation, yoga, or doing a hobby.

Self-care: Make time for yourself regularly and do something that brings you joy. Cultivate your hobbies, meet friends or take a break. By taking care of yourself, you strengthen your mental health.

Set boundaries: As a freelancer, it's important to set clear boundaries. Learn to say no and take time out. Don't overwork yourself and make sure you have enough time for rest and relaxation.

Exchange with others: Seek exchange with other freelancers or like-minded people. Share challenges and experiences and benefit from the experiences of others. The feeling of not being alone can be very helpful.

THE IMPORTANCE OF WORK-LIFE BALANCE

As a freelancer, the boundaries between work and leisure are often blurred. It's important to find a healthy work-life balance to be successful in the long run. Here are some tips that can help you:

Time management: Plan your work well and set realistic goals. Prioritize your tasks and create clear structures. This way, you can keep track of everything and work effectively.

Breaks and recovery: Take regular breaks and allow yourself periods of recovery. Get up in between, take short walks, or relax with a cup of tea. Breaks are important to recharge your batteries and be able to work productively.

Leisure activities: Consciously plan leisure activities that bring you joy. Meet friends, play sports or indulge in your hobbies. By consciously reserving time for yourself and your interests, you create a healthy balance between work and leisure.

Set boundaries: Set clear boundaries between work and play. Define fixed working hours and stick to them. Avoid being available all the time and create clear dividing lines between your work and personal life.

Physical and mental health are crucial factors in your success as a freelancer. By taking care of your health, you can work successfully in the long term and achieve your goals. Take time for yourself, nurture your interests, and maintain a healthy work-life balance. Only if you are healthy can you develop your full potential and work successfully as a freelancer.

WORK-LIFE-BALANCE ALS FREELANCER

As a freelancer, it's often a challenge to find a healthy work-life balance. The flexibility and freedom that comes with self-employment can blur the lines between work and personal life. In this section, we'll look at how you can achieve a good work-life balance as a freelancer to be successful both professionally and personally.

THE IMPORTANCE OF WORK-LIFE BALANCE

A good work-life balance is crucial to be able to work successfully and happily as a freelancer in the long term. It's about finding the right balance between work, family, friends, hobbies, and personal recreation. An unbalanced work-life balance can lead to stress, exhaustion, and burnout, which can negatively impact your productivity and well-being.

THE CHALLENGES OF WORK-LIFE BALANCE AS A FREELANCER

As a freelancer, you often have the freedom to determine your own working hours. On the one hand, this can be very advantageous, as you can flexibly adapt your work to your personal needs. On the other hand, it can also make it difficult for you to draw clear boundaries between work and leisure. It's important to realize that you don't have to work around the clock and that it's also important to have time for yourself and your personal interests.

TIPS FOR A HEALTHY WORK-LIFE BALANCE

To achieve a healthy work-life balance as a freelancer, there are some tips that can help you:

Set clear working hours

Set fixed working hours and stick to them. This means that you work at certain times and at other times you finish your work and focus on your free time. By setting clear boundaries, you can prevent work and personal life from merging.

Create a separate workspace

Set up your own workspace that's separate from your private space. In this way, you create a clear spatial separation between work and leisure. When you enter your workspace, you know it's time to focus on your work. When you leave it, you can switch off and relax.

Schedule regular breaks

Take regular short breaks during work to recover and recharge your batteries. Get up, go for a walk, or do a quick yoga or breathing exercise. These breaks help you clear your mind and can increase your productivity.

Prioritize your tasks

Set clear priorities and focus on the most important tasks. This avoids overload and allows you to focus on what's really important. Also, learn to say no when you already have enough work and can't take on additional projects.

Maintain social contacts

As a freelancer, it's easy to feel isolated and alone. Therefore, maintain your social contacts and seek exchange with other people. Meet up regularly with friends or colleagues, attend networking events, or join a community of freelancers. Sharing with others can not only be inspiring, but it can also help you not feel alone.

Create clear leisure activities

Consciously schedule time for your hobbies and interests. Find activities that bring you joy and relax. This can be sports, reading, painting or other creative activities. By organizing your free time consciously, you can recover better and recharge your batteries.

THE BENEFITS OF A GOOD WORK-LIFE BALANCE

A good work-life balance has many advantages. It allows you to work more productively and efficiently because you are rested and motivated. It also helps you feel physically and mentally healthy. A good work-life balance can also boost your creativity and ability to innovate, as you have room for new ideas and perspectives.

RESULT

A healthy work-life balance is crucial to work successfully and happily as a freelancer in the long term. By setting clear boundaries, scheduling regular breaks, and consciously organizing your free time, you can achieve a good work-life balance. Remember that your health and well-being are just as important as your professional goals and responsibilities.

THE IMPORTANCE OF BREAKS AND RECOVERY

As a freelancer, it's easy to get caught up in the work and neglect the importance of breaks and recovery. But it is precisely these aspects that are crucial for our physical and mental health, as well as for our long-term productivity and satisfaction. In this section, we'll look at the importance of breaks and recovery and give some practical tips on how to incorporate them into your daily work.

WHY BREAKS ARE IMPORTANT

Breaks are not just there to switch off for a short time and recharge your batteries. They are also crucial for our cognitive performance and creativity. Studies have shown that taking regular breaks helps maintain our concentration and improve our ability to think. By recovering regularly, we can also better manage stress and reduce the risk of burnout.

TYPES OF BREAKS

There are different types of breaks that you can incorporate into your workday. Short breaks of a few minutes can help improve your concentration and refresh your mind. These could be short walks, stretching, or just closing your eyes for a few minutes. Longer breaks of 15-30 minutes can be used to relax, grab a bite to eat, or chat with other people. In addition, regular longer breaks of at least an hour or more are important to fully recover and recharge your batteries.

INTEGRATE BREAKS INTO YOUR DAILY WORK ROUTINE

It is important to consciously integrate breaks into your everyday work. Plan them firmly and stick to them. One way to do this is by using time management techniques such as the Pomodoro Technique. This technique involves working at intervals of 25 minutes, followed by a short break of 5 minutes. After four work intervals, you can take a longer break of 15-30 minutes. By using this technique, you can ensure that you take regular breaks and increase your productivity.

ACTIVE RECREATION

Breaks don't have to be just doing nothing. Active recreation can be just as important. This means that you can use your breaks to engage in activities that bring you joy and relax. This can be sports, yoga, meditation, reading or other hobbies. By incorporating active recovery into your breaks, you can not only relax your mind, but also strengthen your body and keep it fit.

THE ROLE OF RECREATION IN CREATIVITY

Recovery also plays an important role in our creativity. Often, the best ideas and solutions come when we relax our minds and switch off. By making time for rest and relaxation on a regular basis, you can boost your creativity and gain new perspectives. Use your breaks to disconnect from work and engage in other things that bring you joy. You'll be surprised how this can affect your creativity.

LEARNING THE RIGHT WAY TO DEAL WITH BREAKS

It can be challenging to learn how to properly manage breaks, especially if you're used to constantly dealing with work. It requires discipline and the ability to let go. Start by consciously scheduling time for breaks and stick to it. Set clear boundaries and allow yourself to recover without feeling guilty. Over time, you will realize that breaks are not only important, but also necessary to be successful and healthy in the long term.

RESULT

Breaks and recovery are crucial for our physical and mental health, as well as our productivity and creativity. By integrating regular breaks into our daily work routine and consciously taking time for recovery, we can increase our performance and reduce the risk of burnout. Use your breaks to relax, recuperate, and boost your creativity. Remember that breaks aren't a waste of time, they're an investment in your long-term health and success as a freelancer.

DEALING WITH STRESS AND BURNOUT PREVENTION

As a freelancer, it is important to develop a healthy way of dealing with stress and prevent burnout. Being self-employed can come with a variety of challenges that can lead to stress. In this section, we will look at different strategies and techniques to reduce stress and prevent burnout.

RECOGNISING AND UNDERSTANDING STRESS

Stress is a natural part of life and can even be helpful in certain situations. However, as a freelancer, chronic stress can lead to exhaustion and burnout. It is important to recognize and understand the signs of stress in order to be able to take timely action.

Some common signs of stress include:

Insomnia

Irritability and mood swings

Concentration problems

Exhaustion and tiredness

Physical ailments such as headaches or stomach problems

It's important to take these signs seriously and respond to them to avoid long-term health effects.

STRESS MANAGEMENT TECHNIQUES

There are several techniques to deal with and manage stress. Everyone is different, so it's important to find the techniques that best suit you. Here are some best practices for managing stress:

Relaxation

Relaxation techniques such as meditation, breathing exercises, and progressive muscle relaxation can help reduce stress and calm the mind.

These techniques can be regularly integrated into everyday life in order to benefit from their effects in the long term.

Sport and physical activity

Regular physical activity can help reduce stress and improve overall well-being. Whether it's yoga, running, swimming, or any other sport, physical activity can help clear your mind and reduce stress.

Time management

Effective time management is crucial to reduce stress. It's important to set realistic goals, prioritize, and schedule breaks. Through good organization and planning, stressful situations can be avoided or at least minimized.

Social support

Sharing with other freelancers or getting support from friends and family can be a great help in reducing stress. Sharing experiences, worries and challenges can have a relieving effect and open up new perspectives.

Hobbies and interests

Pursuing hobbies and interests outside of work can help reduce stress and increase well-being. It is important to find time for yourself and for activities that bring joy and relax the mind.

BURNOUT-PRÄVENTION

Burnout is a state of emotional, mental, and physical exhaustion caused by chronic stress. To prevent burnout, it is important to take care of your own health and well-being. Here are some burnout prevention tips:

Setting boundaries

It's important to draw clear boundaries between work and play. Excessive work and being available all the time can lead to overwork. It is important to consciously take time out and allow yourself time for rest and relaxation.

Self-care

Your own health and well-being should always come first. It is important to eat a balanced diet, get enough sleep and exercise regularly. Maintaining social contacts and pursuing hobbies are also important aspects of self-care.

Setting realistic goals

It's important to set realistic goals and not overextend yourself. The pressure to always be successful can lead to stress and burnout. It's important to set realistic expectations for yourself and not compare yourself to others.

Take time-outs

Regular breaks and vacations are important to reduce stress and recharge your batteries. It's important to consciously take time for rest and relaxation and not feel guilty when you need a break.

Seek professional help

When stress gets out of hand and signs of burnout appear, it's important to seek professional help. A coach or therapist can help identify the causes of stress and burnout and develop appropriate strategies for coping.

Self-employment can be a fulfilling and rewarding experience, but it's important to take care of your own health and well-being. By recognizing and managing stress and preventing burnout, you can stay successful and healthy as a freelancer.

SUCCESS TIPS FOR FREELANCERS

EFFECTIVE SELF-MARKETING

Self-marketing is a crucial factor for success as a freelancer. It's about presenting yourself and your services or products effectively, convincing potential customers, and building long-term business relationships. In this section, we'll share some tips and strategies to help you improve your self-marketing and grow your customer base.

BUILD YOUR OWN BRAND

A strong brand is crucial to stand out from the competition and attract potential customers. It's all about creating a consistent and professional look and feel that reflects your personality and expertise. Here are some steps to building your own brand:

Define your target audience: Think about who your potential customers are and what their needs and problems are. Tailor your message and offer accordingly.

Develop a strong logo and design: An appealing logo and consistent design will add a professional touch to your brand. Make sure your logo and design fit your industry and target audience.

Create a compelling business description: Clearly and concisely describe who you are, the services you offer, and the value you provide to your customers. Use engaging language and highlight your unique selling points.

Use social media: Social media platforms such as LinkedIn, Xing, or Instagram are an excellent way to showcase your brand and connect with potential customers. Regularly maintain your profiles, share relevant content, and network with other experts in your industry.

BUILD A COMPELLING ONLINE PRESENCE

In today's digital world, having a professional and engaging online presence is essential. Potential customers often search online for service providers and find out about their offers and references. Here are some tips for building a compelling online presence:

Create a professional website: Your website is your digital business card. Make sure it's attractively designed, has clear information about your services, and is easy to navigate. Also, show testimonials and customer reviews to build trust.

Optimize your website for search engines: Make sure that your website is easily found in search engines for relevant search terms. Use relevant keywords in your texts, optimize your meta tags, and ensure a fast loading time for your website.

Blog regularly: A blog is a great way to show off your expertise and engage potential customers. Write informative and relevant blog posts on a regular basis on topics that interest your target audience. Also, share your posts on social media to increase your reach.

Use online platforms: There are many online platforms where freelancers can offer their services, such as Upwork, Freelancer, or Fiverr. Use these platforms to attract new customers and increase your reach.

USE NETWORKING AND REFERRALS

A strong network can help you attract new customers and grow your business. Here are some tips on how to network effectively and use referrals:

Attend industry events and meetups: Industry events and meetups are a great way to meet other experts in your industry and meet potential customers. Be active, socialize and exchange ideas with others.

Maintain existing contacts: Stay in touch with your existing customers and business partners. Send regular updates about your work, share relevant information, and ask for recommendations.

Offer incentives for referrals: Reward your customers or business partners when they refer you to new customers. This can be in the form of discounts, vouchers or other perks.

Become a recommender yourself: Recommend other freelancers or service providers if you are convinced of their work. This can lead to a mutual referral culture and open up new business opportunities for you.

SUCCESSFUL ACQUISITION AND CUSTOMER RETENTION

Acquiring new clients and retaining existing clients is critical to success as a freelancer. Here are some tips to improve your prospecting and retention strategies:

Identify potential customers: Research your target audience and identify potential customers who may have a need for your services. Create a list of potential customers and prioritize them based on relevance.

Personalize your approach: Tailor your approach to each prospect individually, show that you have dealt with their company and its challenges, and how you can help them.

Provide value: Make sure you're providing clear value to your potential customers. Show how your services can solve his problems or achieve his goals.

Stay in touch: Keep in touch with your clients, even after a project has been completed. Send regular updates, share relevant information, and ask for feedback.

Provide excellent customer service: Excellent customer service is key to customer loyalty. Always be available, respond quickly to inquiries and make sure your customers are happy with your work.

Use cross-selling and up-selling: Offer additional services or upgrades to your existing customers. This can help increase revenue per customer and build long-term business relationships.

Effective self-marketing is a continuous process that requires time and commitment. Experiment with different strategies, analyze the results, and adjust your approaches accordingly. With the right self-marketing, you can expand your client base and achieve long-term success as a freelancer.

CUSTOMER LOYALTY AND CUSTOMER SERVICE

Customer loyalty and customer service are crucial factors in the success of a freelancer. It's about retaining existing customers in the long term and offering them excellent service. In this section, we'll look at different strategies and techniques to optimize customer retention and customer service.

THE IMPORTANCE OF CUSTOMER LOYALTY

Customer retention is of great importance because it is easier and more cost-effective to retain existing customers than to acquire new ones. Happy clients are more likely to work with a freelancer again and recommend them to others. Therefore, it is important to build a long-term relationship with customers and understand their needs and expectations.

Communication and transparency

Open and transparent communication is the key to customer loyalty. Keep your clients regularly updated on the progress of their projects and inform them of any delays or changes. Be available and respond promptly to inquiries and concerns. Through clear and effective communication, you build trust and show your customers that you care about them.

Individual support

Every customer is unique and has individual needs. Make an effort to respond to each customer's specific requirements and offer customized solutions. Show interest in their projects and take the time to understand their goals and desires. By focusing on the customer and making them feel like they have your full attention, you strengthen customer loyalty.

Measuring customer satisfaction

To measure customer satisfaction, you can get feedback from your customers on a regular basis. Ask them to evaluate your performance and ask for suggestions for improvement. Take criticism seriously and use it to continuously improve your service. By providing regular feedback, you show your customers that their opinion is valued and that you strive to meet their expectations.

OPTIMIZE CUSTOMER SERVICE

Excellent customer service is an essential part of customer loyalty. Here are some tips to optimize your customer service:

Fast response times

Customers expect a quick response to their inquiries and concerns. Make an effort to respond within a short period of time and show your customers that you take their concerns seriously. If you don't have a solution ready right away, let the customer know you're working on a solution and give them a realistic timeline.

Friendliness and professionalism

Always be friendly and professional in your dealings with your customers. Respond to their questions and concerns and show understanding for their needs. Treat your customers respectfully and politely, even if there are any discrepancies. A positive and professional approach strengthens the customer relationship and ensures a pleasant cooperation.

Problem-solving skills

Customers come to you because they are looking for a solution to their problem. Make an effort to solve their problems quickly and effectively. Show creativity and flexibility in finding solutions and offer alternative approaches if necessary. By helping your customers achieve their goals, you become a valuable partner and increase customer satisfaction.

Aftercare and support

Customer service doesn't end with the completion of a project. Offer support to your customers even after the collaboration is complete. Be available to answer questions and help with any problems that arise. With good follow-up support, you show your customers that you are interested in a successful cooperation in the long term.

CUSTOMER LOYALTY THROUGH ADDED VALUE

To strengthen customer loyalty, you can provide additional value to your customers. Here are some ways you can achieve this:

Sharing knowledge

Share your knowledge and expertise with your customers. Give them tips and advice to help them in their work. By sharing relevant information, you position yourself as an expert and build trust. Your customers will appreciate your support and see you as a valuable partner.

Exclusive offers

Offer exclusive offers and discounts to your long-term customers, show them that you value their loyalty and reward them for their long-term cooperation. Exclusive offers make your customers feel valued and more likely to stay loyal to you.

Customer Loyalty Programs

Implement customer loyalty programs to retain your customers for the long term. Reward them for their loyalty and offer them special benefits. Customer loyalty programs can include discounts, bonus points, or exclusive events, for example. Such programs make your customers feel valued and more likely to stay loyal to you.

RESULT

Customer loyalty and customer service are crucial factors in the success of a freelancer. Through open communication, individual attention and excellent customer service, you can build long-term customer relationships and increase customer satisfaction. Offer your customers additional value and reward their loyalty to further strengthen customer loyalty. A satisfied customer is a loyal customer and can get you new business through referrals.

CONTINUING EDUCATION AND PERSONAL DEVELOPMENT

As a freelancer, it's crucial to continuously invest in your education and personal development. In an ever-changing world of work, it's important to keep up with the latest trends and technologies and to constantly evolve in order to remain competitive. In this section, we'll look at different opportunities for upskilling and personal development for freelancers.

FURTHER EDUCATION AND TRAINING

One way to educate yourself and learn new skills is through education and training. There are a variety of courses and seminars that are offered specifically for freelancers. These can take place both online and offline and cover a wide range of topics, such as project management, marketing, communication or technical skills. By attending such trainings, freelancers can expand their knowledge and improve their skills, which helps them achieve better results for their clients.

SELF-STUDY AND ONLINE RESOURCES

In addition to further education and training, there are also many opportunities for self-study and the use of online resources. The internet offers a wealth of information and learning materials that freelancers can use to educate themselves in various fields. There are online courses, tutorials, blogs, podcasts, and much more that can help freelancers learn new skills and expand their knowledge. Self-paced allows freelancers to set their own pace of learning and focus on the areas that are most relevant to their work.

MENTORING AND COACHING

Another approach to personal development as a freelancer is mentoring and coaching. By working with an experienced mentor or coach, freelancers can benefit from their knowledge and experience. A mentor or coach can provide valuable insight and advice to promote professional development and overcome challenges. They can also help set goals and develop an individual development plan. Mentoring and coaching can take place both formally and informally, and can include a long-term relationship or short-term counseling.

NETWORKING AND EXCHANGE WITH OTHER FREELANCERS

Another important aspect of personal development as a freelancer is networking and exchanging ideas with other freelancers. By building a network, freelancers can benefit from the experience and knowledge of others. Networking events, industry meetups, and online communities provide opportunities to connect with like-minded people, make new connections, and learn from the experiences of others. By exchanging ideas with other freelancers, new perspectives can be gained, cooperation opportunities can be discovered, and valuable relationships can be built.

PERSONAL DEVELOPMENT AND WORK-LIFE BALANCE

In addition to professional development, it is also important to develop on a personal level and to find a healthy work-life balance. Freelancers should take time to reflect on their own needs and goals and work on their personal development. This can be done, for example, by reading books, listening to podcasts, practicing meditation, or participating in personal development workshops. A good work-life balance is also crucial to be successful and satisfied as a freelancer in the long term. It's important to make time for recreation, hobbies, and social activities to reduce stress and promote well-being.

Personal development as a freelancer is a continuous process that requires time and commitment. By investing in your education, networking with other freelancers, and working on your personal development, you can improve your skills, create new opportunities, and be successful in the long run. It is important to be open to change and adapt to the challenges of the ever-changing world of work. Through continuous training and personal development, freelancers can advance their professional development and achieve their goals.

NETWORKING AND COOPERATIONS

Networking and collaborations are crucial factors for the success of a freelancer. By building a strong network and collaborating with other professionals, new opportunities can open up and your business can be advanced. In this section, we will look at different aspects of networking and collaborations and provide valuable tips on how to use them effectively.

THE IMPORTANCE OF NETWORKING

Networking is an essential part of being a freelancer. It allows the exchange of knowledge, experience and contacts with other professionals in the sector. Through networking, new orders can be generated, potential customers can be won and long-term business relationships can be established.

To network effectively, it's important to regularly attend industry events, conferences, and meetups. There you can meet like-minded people, exchange ideas with them and get to know potential cooperation partners. It is also advisable to get involved in relevant online communities and social networks to increase your visibility and connect with other freelancers.

Networking isn't just about making connections, it's also about building and maintaining relationships. It's important to be authentic and interested, listening to others and helping them when needed. By building trust and mutual support, long-term collaborations can be created that are mutually beneficial.

COLLABORATIONS WITH OTHER FREELANCERS

There can be many benefits to working with other freelancers. By combining different skills and experiences, joint projects can be implemented that would not be feasible alone. Collaborations also allow freelancers to take on larger assignments and expand their services.

In order to enter into successful collaborations, it is important to find the right partners. Attention should be paid to complementarity, i.e. that the skills and experience of the partners should complement each other. It is also advisable to have common values and goals to ensure long-term cooperation.

When collaborating with other freelancers, clear communication and good organization are crucial. It is important to clarify the expectations and goals of both sides and to create a clear project plan. Regular meetings and updates help monitor the progress of the project and resolve any issues early on.

NETWORKS AND PLATFORMS FOR FREELANCERS

There are various networks and platforms designed specifically for freelancers that facilitate exchange and collaboration. These platforms offer the opportunity to network with other freelancers, find projects, and support each other.

An example of such a platform is LinkedIn. LinkedIn is a professional social network that allows freelancers to showcase their profile, socialize, and find potential clients. By sharing content and engaging in relevant groups, visibility can be increased and the network expanded.

Another platform is Upwork. Upwork is an online platform where freelancers can offer their services and find potential clients. By creating a strong profile and collecting positive reviews, freelancers can increase their chances of getting jobs and open up new business opportunities.

It is advisable to try different platforms and find out which ones best suit your needs and goals. It is also important to be active in these networks, engaging and building relationships to realize the full potential of networking and collaborations.

TIPS FOR SUCCESSFUL NETWORKING AND COLLABORATIONS

Be active: Regularly attend industry events and meetups, get involved in online communities and social networks.

Be authentic: Show interest in others, listen, and help when needed.

Build relationships: Invest time and energy in building long-term relationships based on trust and mutual support.

Find the right partners: Look for freelancers whose skills and experience complement each other, and who share similar values and goals.

Communicate clearly: Clarify the expectations and goals of both sides and create a clear project plan.

Use networks and platforms: Explore different networks and platforms for freelancers and find out which ones suit you best.

Be active in the networks: present yourself, share content and get involved in relevant groups.

Try different platforms: Create a strong profile and collect positive reviews to increase your chances of getting orders.

Networking and collaborations are important tools for the success of a freelancer. By building a strong network and collaborating with other professionals, new opportunities can be unlocked and one's own business can be advanced. Take advantage of these opportunities to take your freelance life to the next level.

COWORKING SPACES AND ALTERNATIVE PLACES OF WORK

PROS AND CONS OF COWORKING SPACES

In recent years, coworking spaces have become a popular alternative for freelancers who no longer want to work alone from home. These shared workplaces offer numerous advantages, but also some disadvantages that need to be taken into account.

ADVANTAGES OF COWORKING SPACES

Community & Networking

One of the biggest benefits of coworking spaces is the opportunity to be part of a community of like-minded people. Here, freelancers can get in touch with other self-employed people, entrepreneurs and creatives, exchange ideas and learn from each other. Networking in coworking spaces often results in new business opportunities, collaborations and projects.

Professional working environment

Coworking spaces offer a professional working environment with modern equipment. Unlike working from home, where there may be distractions and a lack of infrastructure, coworking spaces offer a productive atmosphere. There are usually desks, office chairs, fast internet and often meeting rooms that can be used.

Flexibility and scalability

Another advantage of coworking spaces is flexibility. Freelancers can rent a workspace for a day, a week, or a month, depending on their needs. This allows them to adapt their work environment to their current needs. In addition, many coworking spaces offer the possibility of renting additional workspaces or offices as the company grows.

Synergy effects and inspiration

There is often an inspiring atmosphere in coworking spaces, as people from different industries and with different skills meet in one place. The exchange of ideas and experiences creates synergy effects that can lead to new creative solutions and innovations. The diversity of people and projects in coworking spaces can help freelancers broaden their own horizons and gain new perspectives.

Shared resources and services

Coworking spaces often offer additional resources and services that are available to freelancers. These include, for example, printers, scanners, conference rooms, kitchen areas, and sometimes even gyms or event spaces. By sharing these resources, freelancers can save costs and benefit from better infrastructure.

DISADVANTAGES OF COWORKING SPACES

Cost

The biggest disadvantage of coworking spaces is the cost. Compared to working from home or renting your own office, the rental prices for coworking spaces are often higher. Freelancers must therefore carefully consider whether the additional costs are worth it and whether they are actually taking advantage of the services and benefits offered.

Distractions and noise

Although coworking spaces offer a productive work environment, they can also be associated with distractions and noise. Since many people work in an open space, there may be noises and conversations that interfere with concentration. In addition, it can be difficult to retreat to a coworking space and work undisturbed.

Lack of privacy

Another disadvantage of coworking spaces is the lack of privacy. Since the workstations are often arranged in an open space, there is little room for personal conversations or confidential phone calls. Freelancers who value privacy or handle confidential information should take this into account when choosing a coworking space.

Limited availability

Popular coworking spaces can experience bottlenecks, especially during peak hours. It may happen that all workstations are occupied or that it is difficult to reserve a meeting room. Freelancers should therefore plan well in advance and, if necessary, consider alternative places of work.

Social interaction and distractions

Although community can be an advantage in coworking spaces, it can also lead to social interactions and distractions. It can be tempting to chat with other coworkers or attend events and networking events instead of focusing on your own work. Freelancers, therefore, need to be disciplined and use their time effectively to stay productive.

Overall, coworking spaces offer many benefits for freelancers, including community, networking opportunities, a professional work environment, flexibility, and synergies. However, they also come with costs, distractions, and a lack of privacy. Freelancers should therefore carefully consider whether a coworking space fits their individual needs and working habits.

CHOOSING THE RIGHT WORKPLACE

The right workplace is of great importance for freelancers. While some people are best off working in a quiet office, others prefer the atmosphere of a busy coworking space. The choice of workplace depends on various factors, such as personal preferences, working style and financial possibilities. In this section, we'll look at choosing the right workspace for freelancers and look at different options.

HOME OFFICE

The home office is the first choice for many freelancers. It offers the opportunity to work in your own four walls and be flexible. However, there are a few things to keep in mind to make working from home effective:

A dedicated workspace: It is important to set up a dedicated workspace in the house or apartment. This area should be free of distractions and have enough space for a desk, a comfortable chair, and all the work materials you need.

Structure and routine: When working from home, it's easy to blur the lines between work and play. It's important to have a clear structure and routine to stay productive. This means setting fixed working hours and scheduling breaks.

Minimize distractions: There are many potential distractions when working from home, such as household chores, watching TV, or social media. It's important to minimize these distractions by setting clear rules and disciplining yourself.

Working from home offers many advantages, such as flexibility and cost savings. However, it also requires discipline and self-organization to work effectively.

COWORKING SPACES

Coworking spaces are a popular option for freelancers looking for an alternative work environment. These shared offices offer a variety of benefits:

Networking opportunities: People from different industries and with different skills work in coworking spaces. This offers the opportunity to make contacts, exchange ideas and get to know potential cooperation partners or customers.

Motivation and inspiration: The atmosphere in coworking spaces is often motivating and inspiring. Working alongside other creative and committed people can increase one's productivity and encourage new ideas.

Infrastructure and equipment: Coworking spaces usually offer a modern infrastructure and a variety of amenities such as fast internet, printers, meeting rooms, and kitchen areas.

Flexibility: Coworking spaces often offer flexible membership options that allow freelancers to rent a workspace based on their needs. This is especially beneficial for freelancers who don't need to work in the office every day.

However, it's important to note that coworking spaces come at a cost. Depending on the location and amenities, prices may vary. It is advisable to compare the different options and choose the one that best suits your needs and budget.

ALTERNATIVE PLACES OF WORK

In addition to the home office and coworking spaces, there are other alternative places of work available to freelancers. Here are some examples:

Cafes and libraries: Many freelancers like to work in cafes or libraries to have a different environment and disconnect from home or the office. These places often offer a quiet atmosphere and a great way to focus.

Public parks: When the weather is nice, working outdoors in a public park can be a pleasant change. It offers the opportunity to get some fresh air and enjoy nature while being productive.

Rentable offices: There are companies that offer offices for rent that are specifically designed for freelancers and small businesses. These offices often offer a professional working environment and the opportunity to interact with other professionals.

Working groups: In some cities, there are working groups that allow freelancers to share a workspace. This can be a cost-effective option and provides an opportunity to interact with other freelancers and learn from each other.

Choosing the right workplace depends on individual needs and preferences. It's important to try different options and find out which workplace best suits your way of working.

RESULT

Choosing the right workplace is an important factor in success as a freelancer. Whether it's a home office, a coworking space or an alternative place of work, every freelancer should choose the workplace that best suits their needs and working style. It's important to weigh the pros and cons of each option and choose the one that best promotes productivity and well-being.

ALTERNATIVE PLACES OF WORK FOR FREELANCERS

As a freelancer, you have the freedom to choose your own workplace. While coworking spaces are a popular option, there are other alternative work venues you can consider. In this section, we'll take a closer look at some of these options.

HOME OFFICE

Working from home is one of the most popular options for freelancers. It gives you the opportunity to work from the comfort of your own home while enjoying the benefits of flexible working hours and familiar surroundings. You can set up your own workspace and design it according to your needs. It's important to have a separate room that serves as your office to separate work and personal life. Working from home gives you the opportunity to work in a quiet and focused environment without being distracted by others.

CAFES AND LIBRARIES

If you're looking for a change from your home office, you can also work in cafes or libraries. These places offer a pleasant atmosphere and a certain background noise that can be inspiring for some freelancers. You can get your work done while sipping a coffee or getting inspired by the tranquil surroundings of a library. However, it's important to respect the etiquette of these places and make sure you can maintain enough focus and productivity.

PARK OR BEACH

If you like to work outside and enjoy nature, you can also work in parks or on the beach. These places offer a relaxed and inspiring environment that can encourage your creativity. You can get your work done while enjoying the fresh air and beautiful surroundings. However, it is important that you make sure that you have a reliable internet connection and that you protect your work materials to avoid possible damage from the weather.

COMMUNITY CENTERS AND LIBRARIES

Some community centers and libraries offer dedicated workspaces for freelancers. These places are often equipped with desks, chairs, and a reliable internet connection. They provide a quiet and productive environment where you can get your work done. Another advantage of these places is that you have the opportunity to meet and exchange ideas with other freelancers and self-employed people. This can lead to new collaboration opportunities and networking opportunities.

RENTABLE OFFICES OR WORKSPACES

If you want a dedicated workspace outside of your home, you can also rent offices or workspaces. There are various providers who offer flexible leases for offices or workspaces. These rooms are often equipped with all the necessary facilities, such as desks, chairs, internet connection and meeting rooms. Renting an office or workspace can provide you with a professional work environment and help you focus better on your work.

TRAVEL AND WORK

As a freelancer, you have the opportunity to work from anywhere. You can use this freedom to travel and get your work done at the same time. You can work in different places and gain new inspiration. It's important to make sure you have a reliable internet connection and that you keep your work materials safe and secure. Working while traveling requires good organization and time management to ensure you can get your work done on time.

SUMMARY

There are many alternative places to work for freelancers. Whether you prefer to work from home, in cafes or libraries, outside in parks or on the beach, in community centers or libraries, in rented offices or workspaces, or while traveling, the choice of work location is entirely up to you. It's important to choose a place where you feel comfortable and can work productively. Experiment with different places to work and see which one works best for you. Remember that flexibility and adaptability are important qualities for freelancers to be successful.

OUTLOOK AND FUTURE PROSPECTS

FURTHER DEVELOPMENT AS A FREELANCER

As a freelancer, it's important to continuously evolve in order to be successful and keep up with the changes in the world of work. Progression as a freelancer includes both personal and professional development. In this section, we'll cover various aspects of development and give tips on how to expand your skills and knowledge as a freelancer.

CONTINUING EDUCATION AND PERSONAL DEVELOPMENT

One of the most important ways to grow as a freelancer is through continuous education. The world of work is constantly changing, and it's important to keep up with the latest trends and technologies. By attending seminars, workshops, or online courses, freelancers can expand their knowledge and learn new skills.

In addition, it is also important to develop personally. As a freelancer, you are not only in demand for your professional skills, but also for your soft skills. Communication skills, time management, self-organization, and problem-solving skills are just a few examples of soft skills that are critical to success as a freelancer. Through the targeted development of these skills, one can increase one's professionalism and effectiveness.

NETWORKING AND COOPERATIONS

Another important aspect of developing as a freelancer is networking. By building a network, you can not only get to know potential clients, but also learn from other freelancers and support each other. Networking events, industry meetings, or online communities offer opportunities to socialize and connect with other freelancers.

In addition, collaborations with other freelancers or companies can be a great way to develop yourself. By collaborating with others, you can benefit from their experience and knowledge and gain new perspectives. Joint projects can also help to expand one's own portfolio and win new customers.

SELF-MARKETING AND BRANDING

As a freelancer, it's important to market yourself and build a strong personal brand. A professional online presence, such as a well-designed website or a strong portfolio, can help convince potential customers and showcase your expert knowledge.

In addition, it is important to be clear about your own strengths and unique selling points and to communicate them in a targeted manner. Clear branding and positioning can help you stand out from the competition and attract potential customers.

FLEXIBILITY AND ADAPTABILITY

The world of work is constantly changing, and as a freelancer, it's important to be flexible and adaptable. New technologies, trends and customer requirements require continuous adaptation of one's own skills and way of working.

Flexibility also means being open to new opportunities and not being limited to a specific niche or clientele. By being willing to take on new challenges and develop in other areas as well, you can increase your chances of success as a freelancer.

THE BALANCE BETWEEN STABILITY AND INNOVATION

As a freelancer, it's important to find a balance between stability and innovation. Stability means relying on proven ways of working and customer relationships, while innovation means coming up with new ideas and approaches.

It is important to regularly question yourself and check whether the previous way of working is still effective or whether there are opportunities to improve. At the same time, however, you should also build on what is already successful and not constantly hunt for new trends and technologies.

Growing as a freelancer is a continuous process that requires time and commitment. By continuously educating yourself, expanding your network, marketing yourself, and staying flexible, you can maximize your chances of success as a freelancer and successfully adapt to changes in the world of work.

INDUSTRY TRENDS AND CHANGES

The world of work is in a constant state of change, and the freelance industry is not unaffected. In this section, we'll take a look at the current industry trends and changes that freelancers can expect in the future.

DIGITALIZATION AND AUTOMATION

Digitalization has already changed many areas of our lives and will continue to have a major impact on the world of work. More and more tasks are being automated, which means that certain activities for freelancers may be eliminated or will change significantly. It is therefore important to familiarize yourself with the new technologies and to continuously educate yourself in order to remain competitive.

SUSTAINABILITY AND SOCIAL RESPONSIBILITY

Another important trend in the world of work is the increasing importance of sustainability and social responsibility. More and more companies are attaching importance to environmentally friendly and socially responsible business practices. Freelancers who specialize in these topics or can offer appropriate solutions have a good chance of standing out from the competition and attracting new clients.

REMOTE WORK AND VIRTUAL TEAMS

The ability to work from anywhere is becoming increasingly popular. Remote work and virtual teams allow freelancers to collaborate with clients and colleagues regardless of their location. This trend is expected to continue to intensify as companies realize that this allows them to access a larger talent pool while saving costs. Freelancers should therefore familiarize themselves with the tools and technologies needed to collaborate in virtual teams.

CHANGES IN WORK CULTURE

The traditional 9-to-5 work culture is increasingly being replaced by more flexible working models. More and more companies are offering their employees the opportunity to organize their own working hours and work from home or other locations. These changes also have an impact on freelancers, as they can work more flexibly and adapt better to the needs of their clients. However, it is important not to lose sight of the balance between work and leisure and to set clear boundaries.

SPECIALIZATION AND NICHE MARKETS

With the increasing competition in the freelance industry, it is becoming increasingly important to specialize in a particular niche. Customers are increasingly looking for experts who have specific expertise and can offer tailor-made solutions. Freelancers should therefore continuously develop their skills and knowledge and focus on specific industries or areas of responsibility.

CHANGES IN THE WAY WE WORK WITH CUSTOMERS

The way freelancers collaborate with their clients is also changing. More and more companies are relying on project-based collaboration and hiring freelancers for specific tasks or projects. This opens up new opportunities for freelancers, as they can work more flexibly and focus on their strengths. At the same time, however, this also requires good self-marketing and the ability to quickly adapt to new teams and projects.

EVOLVING THE GIG ECONOMY

The gig economy, i.e. the mediation of short-term orders and projects, is expected to continue to grow. More and more companies are relying on freelancers to be able to react flexibly to their needs. This provides freelancers with the opportunity to work on different projects and in different industries and continuously expand their network. At the same time, however, the gig economy also requires good self-organization and the ability to adapt quickly to new tasks.

IMPACT OF THE COVID-19 PANDEMIC

The COVID-19 pandemic has permanently changed the world of work and will continue to have an impact in the future. Many companies have adapted their way of working to the new realities and are increasingly relying on remote work and virtual collaboration. This also has an impact on freelancers, as the demand for certain services has changed. It is important to remain flexible and adapt to the new requirements.

The freelance industry is dynamic and subject to constant change. It is therefore important to keep up to date with current industry trends and changes and to continuously evolve. By adapting and staying flexible, you can successfully move into the future as a freelancer.

THE IMPORTANCE OF FLEXIBILITY AND ADAPTABILITY

Flexibility and adaptability are two crucial qualities that are of great importance to freelancers. In an ever-changing world of work and in a market characterized by innovation and new technologies, it is essential to be flexible and adapt to new realities. In this section, we'll take a closer look at why these traits are so important and how they can help ensure long-term success as a freelancer.

FLEXIBILITY AS THE KEY TO SUCCESS

Flexibility is a quality that allows freelancers to quickly adapt to new situations and adapt to changing requirements. As a freelancer, you are often faced with unforeseen challenges, whether it's a short-term assignment that needs to be completed or a change in the client's requirements. In such situations, it is important to be flexible and willing to adapt.

A flexible way of working also allows freelancers to respond to changes in the market. New trends and technologies can influence the demand for certain services. By staying flexible and willing to learn new skills or adapt your offering, you can ensure that you remain relevant and competitive.

In addition, flexibility also allows for a better work-life balance. As a freelancer, you often have the freedom to determine your own working hours. This opens up the opportunity to better reconcile work and personal obligations and to lead a balanced life.

ADAPTABILITY AS THE KEY TO INNOVATION

Adaptability is closely linked to flexibility, but it goes a step further. While flexibility refers to the ability to adapt to new situations, adaptability refers to the ability to proactively address change and drive innovation.

As a freelancer, it's important to be open to change and willing to break new ground. The world of work is constantly evolving, and to be successful, you have to be willing to adapt and explore new opportunities. This can mean learning new technologies, entering new markets, or trying out new business models.

Adaptability also allows freelancers to cater to client needs and offer customized solutions. By adapting to each client's unique needs and being willing to adapt, you can build long-term client loyalty and further expand your success as a freelancer.

THE BENEFITS OF FLEXIBILITY AND ADAPTABILITY

Flexibility and adaptability offer a variety of benefits for freelancers. Here are some of the most important ones:

Competitiveness: Flexibility and adaptability allow you to stay relevant and adapt to changing market conditions. This allows one to remain competitive and take advantage of new business opportunities.

Customer loyalty: By adapting to each customer's individual needs and requirements, you can build strong customer loyalty. Customers appreciate being flexible and willing to adapt to achieve their goals.

Ability to innovate: Flexibility and adaptability allow you to come up with new ideas and offer innovative solutions. This can help differentiate yourself from the competition and open up new business opportunities.

Work-life balance: Flexibility allows freelancers to adjust their working hours to their personal needs and lead a balanced life. This can lead to a better work-life balance and higher satisfaction.

Resilience: Through flexibility and adaptability, you develop a high level of resilience to changes and setbacks. You are better able to deal with challenges and recover quickly.

TIPS FOR DEVELOPING FLEXIBILITY AND ADAPTABILITY

Flexibility and adaptability are qualities that can be developed and improved. Here are some tips on how to strengthen these qualities:

Openness to change: Be open to new ideas and changes. Think of change as an opportunity, not a threat.

Learn continuously: Stay curious and continuously learn new skills. This allows you to adapt to new requirements and evolve.

Network: Connect with other freelancers and professionals in your industry. The exchange of experiences and ideas can help to gain new perspectives and develop further.

Be proactive: Actively approach change and look for new opportunities. Be prepared to take risks and break new ground.

Stay flexible: Adapt your way of working to the needs of your customers and be ready to adapt. Be prepared to learn new technologies and adapt your offering to stay relevant.

Cultivate a positive attitude: A positive attitude helps you deal with change and challenges. See change as an opportunity and believe in your ability to adapt and succeed.

Flexibility and adaptability are crucial qualities that help freelancers succeed in an ever-changing world of work. By staying flexible and willing to adapt, you can take advantage of new opportunities and ensure long-term success.

THE BALANCE BETWEEN STABILITY AND INNOVATION

As a freelancer, it's important to find a balance between stability and innovation. On the one hand, you need stability to build a solid foundation for your business and be successful in the long term. On the other hand, it is also crucial to innovate and adapt to the ever-changing demands of the market. In this section, we will look at how to achieve this balance.

THE IMPORTANCE OF STABILITY

Stability is an important factor for success as a freelancer. It gives you a sense of security and allows you to make long-term plans. Here are some aspects that can contribute to stability:

Financial stability

A solid financial foundation is essential to be successful as a freelancer. It is important to earn a decent income and have reserves for unforeseen expenses. Good accounting and effective financial management are of great importance here.

Retention

Loyalty to existing customers is another factor that contributes to stability. It's easier to work with existing customers than it is to constantly acquire new customers. Through good customer service and the fulfilment of customer wishes, long-term business relationships can be built and thus a stable order situation can be guaranteed.

Efficient workflows

Efficient workflows also contribute to stability. By optimizing and automating your work processes, you can save time and increase your productivity. This allows one to process more orders and thus earn a stable income.

THE IMPORTANCE OF INNOVATION

In addition to stability, innovation is also a decisive factor for success as a freelancer. The ability to adapt to ever-changing market conditions and develop new ideas is of great importance. Here are some aspects that can contribute to innovation:

Continuing education and personal development

In order to innovate, it is important to continuously educate yourself and familiarize yourself with new technologies and trends. By attending trainings, conferences and workshops, you can expand your knowledge and learn new skills. This allows one to offer innovative solutions and stand out from the competition.

Creativity and flexibility

Creativity and flexibility are also important qualities to be innovative. By being open to new ideas and willing to break new ground, you can develop innovative solutions and adapt to changing market conditions. It is important not to rest on one's laurels, but to constantly look for new opportunities.

Networking and Cooperations

Networking and collaborations are other ways to innovate. By exchanging ideas with other freelancers and professionals, you can gain new perspectives and benefit from their experiences and ideas. Joint projects and collaborations can lead to innovative solutions and open up new business opportunities.

FINDING THE BALANCE

Finding the balance between stability and innovation can be challenging. It requires careful planning and continuous adaptation to changing market conditions. Here are some tips that can help you achieve that balance:

Setting long-term goals

Set long-term goals and develop a plan to achieve them. This will give you a clear direction and help you create stability. At the same time, however, you should be flexible enough to adjust your goals as market conditions change.

Continuous training

Invest in your personal and professional development. Keep up to date with new technologies and trends and expand your skills. This allows you to innovate and adapt to the changing demands of the market.

Networking and Cooperation

Cultivate your professional network and look for opportunities to collaborate with other freelancers and professionals. The exchange of ideas and experiences can lead to innovative solutions and open up new business opportunities.

Flexibility and adaptability

Be flexible and willing to adapt to changing market conditions. Be open to new ideas and break new ground when needed. This allows you to innovate and stand out from the competition.

Finding the balance between stability and innovation is critical to success as a freelancer. By creating a solid foundation and at the same time being open to new ideas and changes, you can be successful in the long term and face the challenges of the market.